GEORGE BERNARD SHAW

Sketched from Life

By

EDMUND J. SULLIVAN

January 17, 1929

By permission of *Everyman*

The
REAL BERNARD SHAW

BY

MAURICE COLBOURNE

BOSTON
BRUCE HUMPHRIES, Inc.
PUBLISHERS

PRINTED BY THE COLONIAL PRESS INC.,
CLINTON, MASSACHUSETTS

CONTENTS

THE REAL BERNARD SHAW

SEEING a photograph of Bernard Shaw for the first time, people are apt to imagine him gloriously and patriarchically old. Anybody with such a white beard must be old. In this they are wrong, for he was born as recently as 1856, as his youthful manner and the spring in his step will testify.

He is an Irishman, the son of a Protestant merchant and a musical mother. Packed off to school like any other boy, the school and he had little use for each other and he paid scant attention to his lessons. This touch of nature makes most of us kin to the boy Shaw, but it must not be supposed that he was lazier than most other boys. He was Irish; he was quick to apprehend what would and what would not be useful to him in life; and stored away inside was a capacity for educating himself in his own good time and in his own sweet way. For instance, when it was suggested to him quite recently that he had "gained far more from listening to his mother and her friends singing Mozart than from all his reading put together," his answer was an affirmative "Hooray!"

Disgusted with school and discontented with the

quill-driving for a land agent that followed it, the youth left Ireland for London, to conquer England and the world. At first his progress was hardly triumphal. No one applauded the thin figure that disappeared into the British Museum almost daily for a number of years, to read. To read, read, read. He was an accumulator charging himself with facts, and storing them for long years of use in his verbal batteries. The foundation of Shaw's success in debate was laid in the British Museum. His smiling cocksureness in argument is not bluff, but a cloak for a vast array of relevant facts. If he is courteous in debate it is because he can afford to be; and if he always has the last word it is because he always has a few more facts up his sleeve than his opponent. Reading at the British Museum, however, while an excellent investment, pays no dividends at the time, and the amount of Bernard Shaw's earnings at this time ought to make budding authors pause—or, perhaps, do anything but pause. During his first nine years in London his pen brought him the sum of six pounds, five of which were for a patent medicine advertisement. Shaw in this period, doing what every literary genius has to do some time, wrote his first novel, which nobody would publish. So he wrote another, with the same result. Then another and another and yet another; five novels in all, and not a penny earned. Six years of dogged trying and unbroken failure. Eventually the mice made the acquaintance of the fifty times rejected manuscripts. "But even they," Shaw adds, "were unable to finish them."

Then he gave up novel writing, and became a critic of music and pictures, about which, thanks to his musical mother and the Dublin National Gallery, he knew enough to qualify him. On the then new *Star* and the now extinct *World* in its palmiest days under Edmund Yates he made his mark. Later on he criticized the theater in *The Saturday Review* under Frank Harris.

Thus he escaped from the penury of his novel writing days. He was nearer forty than thirty when he discovered that he could write plays. A lucrative success with his one melodrama, *The Devil's Disciple,* produced in New York by Richard Mansfield, made him rich enough to give up regular journalism and marry a lady of considerable independent means.

In his description of the wedding there is the Shavian touch: "I was very ill when I was married, altogether a wreck on crutches and in an old jacket which the crutch had worn to rags. I had asked my friends, Graham Wallas and Henry Salt, the biographer of Shelley and de Quincey, to act as witnesses; and, of course, in honour of the occasion they were dressed in their best clothes. The registrar never imagined I could possibly be the bridegroom: he took me for the inevitable beggar who completes all wedding processions. Wallas, who was considerably over six feet high, seemed to him to be the hero of the occasion; and he was proceeding calmly to marry him to my betrothed, when Wallas, thinking the formula rather strong for a mere witness, hesitated at the last moment and left the prize to me." In its results this marriage has been as unobtrusive as its actual ceremony was bizarre. Indeed, you will hear many people exclaim, "Oh! *is* there a Mrs. Shaw?" This I consider a high compliment to both of them when you realize how in these days so many of the world's so-called famous men and women parade, exploit, capitalize and sell to the mob details—and the more unsavory or lurid, the higher the price—of their domestic life, or rather lack of it.

As a critic in the theater Bernard Shaw had been dreadfully bored with the kind of play his profession forced him to go and see. He said so frankly. Week by week his pen was pitted against, not the stage's failures, but its darlingest successes, against the very rage and fashion of the day, to wit, the "well made" play of the Scribe—Sardou pattern. The characters in these plays are not real people, he declared. The heroes are nothing but heroic and the villains nothing but villainous! Show me in real life a villain who has not some finer moments or a hero without his weak spot. If this is what you call Romance, I'm out to kill it. True romance has its roots in real life, but this thing the stage serves up is a false romanticism because it has no connection with actuality. In short, the artificial "well made" play was to Shaw what history is to Henry Ford: Bunk. There was only one way of converting satisfied Victorians to his view, and Bernard Shaw took it. He began to write plays himself. And now, fifty years later, he is still at it.

Shaw has told us what he considers is the quintessence of playwriting and its object. The beginning and end of a playwright's job, he says, should be to make the audience believe that they are watching "real things happening to real people." The only man who qualified on these grounds for Shaw's whole-hearted approval was Ibsen, and Shaw has been called "The Laughing Ibsen." The Norwegian, of course, was already an established novelty when the Irishman was aspiring to recognition, and it was perhaps inevitable, however ridiculous, that the younger man should be accused of stealing his ideas from the elder. Ridiculous, because we are not in the habit of saying that Lenin, for instance, "stole" his ideas from Marx. Lenin naturally used what Marx had given the world, and ought to have been ashamed of himself if he hadn't; for what are ideas for except to propagate themselves in other men's minds and bear further fruit there? Shaw was a "follower" of Ibsen, and Lenin of Marx, for the simple reason that they were born later. The truth is, of course, the drama was ready both for Ibsen and for Shaw, and the new force used two men for its practically simultaneous expression. At the beginning of the present century one of these charges against Shaw was hotly contested in the newspapers, the specific charge being that Shaw had taken his ideas from Ibsen, Nietzsche and Schopenhauer. Everybody who was anybody entered the arena for or against, and for a long time the only person who seemed uninterested was Mr. Shaw. At length he, too, made his contribution to the fracas. He rebuked the illiterate English theater critics who, whenever they met with an unfamiliar idea, thought it must come from abroad, although it would have stared them in the face if they had ever opened an English book of any importance. Then he described the street in which he lived, he described his neighbors, their habits, the sanitary accommodation for washerwomen, the vestry on which he sat, the men who made up the committee and how their ideals prevented them from descending so low as to think about washerwomen at all, and concluded: "If a dramatist living in a world like this has got to go to books for his ideas and his inspiration he must be both blind and deaf. Most dramatists are."

The foregoing passage ended the controversy, but for us to-day it does more. It reveals a different Shaw from any touched on yet; a Shaw interested in washer-women, not for their dramatic values so much as for themselves; a Shaw interested in humanity and consequently in the social organization, or rather, as he would put it, the tangle it has got itself into. Shaw the dramatist draws his inspiration from Shaw the social reformer, and in even the skimpiest sketch of him we must at least enumerate Shaw the socialist, Shaw the borough councilor, the vestryman, the tub-thumper, the economist, the pamphleteer, the debater, and must add these to what we already know of the self-educated, married, rich, witty, musical Irishman, lately journalist and critic, now a dramatist in practice these fifty years.

Pray let this dram of biography suffice, and let us leave Bernard Shaw writing his next play at his country home in Hertfordshire, or in his London flat overlooking old Father Thames on its north bank, within a few yards of the site of the stage in White-hall Palace on which Will Shakespeare acted in his own plays before King James.

I do not know Bernard Shaw well; I know no one who does; I know *of* no one who does; and I see no particular reason why Bernard Shaw should know Bernard Shaw particularly well. He can never get a bird's-eye or an impersonal view of himself, that's certain. And so, if in spite of this we still want to play at "Hunt the Shaw," we had better assume, as in other cases, that the works proclaim the man. In that event the procedure is clear: see his plays and read his prefaces and books. It is entirely up to you, dear reader, and I cannot help beyond reminding you that the box offices and the bookshops are open, and that both of them are willing to take your money. None the less, perhaps I can offer you a warning.

Don't look for whole chunks of the real Shaw in any one character, but look rather for fragments and flashes of him in almost all the characters. If you come across a character who fits Bernard Shaw like a glove, be wary of your find. For instance, you might think you had spotted your man in Larry Doyle of *John Bull's Other Island*. What simpler? Irish, son of a small land-agent, Larry was discontented in Ireland: so was Shaw. Larry went to England and made a success there: so did Shaw. But such similarities are superficial, and besides, if Shaw is Larry, what of Peter Keegan? For Keegan and Larry are always at loggerheads, yet without a shadow of doubt Keegan is many times the true mouthpiece of Shaw. Shaw, for example, has no use for cut flowers in his room, and we find Peter Keegan admonishing Nora: "Don't pluck that little flower; if it was a baby you wouldn't want to pull its head off and stick it in a vase of water to look at." Remember, too, Keegan talks more than anyone else at the end of the play and bows himself out with the last word

of the argument—a Shavian life habit. Again, just
as the most obvious points of a Larry Doyle may
prove false scents, so, conversely, the quarry may sometimes be tracked to the most unexpected lairs. Thus,
who would suspect the real Shaw of speaking through
the mouth of Don Juan of *Man and Superman?* Yet
he does, and the sensuous lips of the sixteenth century
libertine and ladies' darling fervently utter a full and
profound exposition of Bernard Shaw's religious and
philosophical convictions. Listen to this: "My brain
labors at a knowledge which does nothing for me
personally but make my body bitter to me and my
decay and death a calamity. Were I not possessed with
a purpose beyond my own, I had better be a ploughman than a philosopher; for the ploughman lives as
long as the philosopher, eats more, sleeps better, and re-
joices in the wife of his bosom with less misgiving."
Or to this piece of ardent, stark sincerity—"I tell you
that as long as I can conceive something better than
myself I cannot be easy unless I am striving to bring
it into existence or clearing the way for it. That is
the law of my life." These two passages form part
of a conversation which occupies more than forty
pages of small print, but it should be said in extenua-
tion that the pow-wow is supposed to take place in
hell, where time, as we know it, is non-existent. All
the same I am sure Don Juan must have taken a
little time to think things over and acquire his

Shavian convictions. Whether such dialogue is dramatic, or such scenes drama, is, of course, a matter of opinion. Personally, I am satisfied with a very easy test. I go and count the box office receipts. Now, if Shaw had been foolish or sanguine enough to tout round the manuscript of the Hell scene among the London theater managers, expecting them to produce it, he would have been informed that no audience would stand for it, because, like Polonius' beard, it was too long: only they would have left out Polonius' beard. But audiences do stand for it. For them it is not too long, and it is a fact that whenever and wherever the Hell scene is incorporated in *Man and Superman* the box office takings increase appreciably. I therefore declare it drama.

But to return to Hunt the Shaw. Here is another tip. In your perusal of the plays, when you meet a character who is considered mad by all the other characters, make a note of him or her; he or she is worth watching. Ten to one the real Shaw is lurking in the very words which caused their speaker to be thought mad. You will find the epithet "mad" applied to any character in the plays who drops bombs of shattering common sense to resolve a social situation rendered ticklish through the other characters abiding by the etiquette of an artificial way of living. The epithet is also applied to anyone who, in suggesting a remedy, thinks only of the benefit of its result instead of the propriety of its application. The reason being, that the commonsensical and the obvious and the true are among the first things to be overlaid and stifled by the layers of custom and prejudice in which man has become encrusted, and the average man, compelled to face these comparative strangers, finds he cannot look them in the eye or follow them, and so denies them. In short, the truthmonger must be called mad lest he embarrass society, and the man who would act on his truthmongering must be put away lest he wreck it. *Saint Joan* exemplifies each in turn. Nearly every character in the play calls the Maid mad, and when she had acted with effect she was put away. In these circumstances the great number of such "mad" persons in the plays is understandable, but nevertheless surprising. Peter Keegan is thought mad by the whole village, which has built up legends to support its opinion. In *Candida,* which is an epic of hometruth-telling, four out of a total of six characters are called mad in the course of the play. Larry Doyle's father considers Tom Broadbent "not quite right in his head." Probably Shaw's own attitude towards these pet madmen of his is best summed up in *Saint Joan* when de Poulengey, urging that the Maid be sent to the Dauphin, says: "We want a few mad people now. See where the sane ones have landed us!"

One other point is worth mentioning. This "reasonable, patient, consistent, apologetic, laborious person, with the temperament of a schoolmaster and the pursuits of a vestryman" (as Shaw has described himself) possesses an intellectual grasp of a situation so embracing, and a human understanding of its victims so sensitive, that he endows his characters impartially with an equal strength, and in this way a keen sense of fairness permeates his work. The preacher and artist are at one. Speaking of his characters, Shaw has said that, for the dramatic moment, he is that character. That is to say, in writing words for his puppets to utter he gives each in turn 100 per cent support. This is magnificently Olympian, but it makes Hunt the Shaw a difficult game. Clues, therefore, are more plentiful in the Prefaces than in the Plays.

IS BERNARD SHAW CONCEITED?

THERE are many questions concerning Shaw which set people by the ears and split any group of them into opposing camps. In this brief study we have space to deal with only three of them. "Is Bernard Shaw Conceited?" "Has Bernard Shaw Changed?" and "Is Bernard Shaw Serious?" Those who, not knowing Bernard Shaw personally, answer the question "Is Bernard Shaw Conceited?" with a "Yes" should be asked this further question: "Would not a man with Bernard Shaw's qualifications and attainments be an unblushing hypocrite and humbug if he pretended to hold a poor opinion of himself?" If Shaw's healthy opinion of himself offends the canons of gentlemanly conduct, he cannot help it; he would rather be "ungentlemanly" than a humbug. Indeed, Shaw gives it as his opinion that no true artist can be a gentleman. "I am," he adds, "an artist."

Consider, too, Bernard Shaw's life and especially his beginnings. He comes to a strange country; he is penniless; his outlook is a cross between that of a boxer and a missionary; he has his bread and butter to earn; he has a point of view which he honestly thinks ought to be heard. Remembering the fate of his five novels, how should he proceed? For he was determined not to spend his life, if he could help it, in providing nesting material for mice. The answer need not surprise us who have grown up with twentieth century methods. He decided to do what every successful man and woman does and has to do to-day; in a word, to advertise. Having no money, the only capital he had to advertise his wares with was himself. Accordingly, the man Bernard Shaw, in cold business blood, engaged the wit Bernard Shaw to advertise the philosopher-preacher Bernard Shaw, and the fact that the wit rather liked his new job only made the engagement a shrewder stroke of business. Shaw has packed these considerations into the following remark: "The spontaneous recognition of really original work begins with a mere handful of people and propagates itself so slowly that it has become a commonplace to say that genius, demanding bread, is given a stone until after its possessor's death. The remedy for this is sedulous advertisement. Accordingly I have advertised myself so well that I find myself, still in middle life, almost as legendary as the Flying Dutchman."

Bernard Shaw's success as a salesman argues not conceit, but wisdom in the choice of his policy, and impish courage, which he no doubt enjoyed displaying, in carrying it through. Is the manufacturer conceited because he tells you that his soaps or his cigarettes or his razors or his whatnots are positively the best in the world? Do we think him bombastic because he spends large sums yearly in blowing his own trumpet? Do we find him insufferable because he dins into us the superlative qualities of his goods from hoardings in all colors and sizes of screaming print? Of course not. We congratulate him, and in England, if he is successful enough, the king makes him a peer of the realm. It does not seem to me fair to admire the manufacturer and condemn the philosopher; both have goods to sell, the only question being how best to sell them, and in realizing the value of advertisement Bernard Shaw only anticipated the approved ways of modern Big Business. But he strenuously denies that he has ever had time to practice what he preaches in this respect, and declares that half his work is unknown to the public for lack of advertisement.

Howbeit, he was always brilliant at the job. He could charm publicity out of an eggshell. His beard, his diet, a cold, the tailoring of his coat, moving house, nothing is too trivial for grist to his publicity mill. Even the brickbats thrown at him he makes use of if so minded, tossing them back envenomed in wit, so that his assailants find they have been throwing boomerangs.

The greatest thing in Shaw's favor was his being an Irishman, for the English would never dream of letting an Englishman talk to them the way Shaw does, insulting them and treating them as children and trying to lead them by the nose. The truth is, the English don't in the least mind foreigners and outsiders criticizing or even leading them. This is a curious trait in a conquering race, and I sometimes suspect the reason of it is, that deep down the English are aware of an innate superiority over all the other nations of the earth; therefore they say, "Let the foreign critics castigate and harangue us to their heart's content, we shall not take what they say too seriously. Let the foreign leaders stand to the wheel of the Ship of State, in peace or war, we will aboard too, sure in the knowledge that our native seamanship will bring us safely to port in the long run." Be this as it may, it is worth noting that it was an Irishman who led the troops to victory in Napoleon's wars; that an Irishman followed by a Scotsman led in the Great War; that a professing Jew, Benjamin Disraeli, first conceived the British Empire as we know it to-day, and won the romantic co-operation of a Queen who could not bear the sight of her foursquare English Gladstone; that the English Asquith was deposed in favor of the Welsh Lloyd George by an English newspaper controlled by a Canadian; that even when it was an Englishman, Baldwin, who turned Lloyd George out, it was a Scotch Canadian who succeeded him; while the leader of the Labor Party and its first Prime Minister is a Scotsman. It is, then, only part of a general national anomaly that the English suffer the Irish Bernard Shaw to settle in their midst and set himself up as Public Thinker.

As a publicity merchant Shaw tickled the public's palate so successfully that it kept on, and keeps on, asking for more, although for years past he has been in no commercial need of limelight. It is the public's fault; we refuse to let him retire from his publicity business; we make him work even when he is ill, squeezing "copy" from his sickbed. You will remember how each summer, when Bernard Shaw goes holidaying somewhere on the Mediterranean or in the Italian Lakes, the newspapers of the world fairly burst into pictures of him in all kinds of postures and clothes and lack of clothes. We really cannot hold Shaw responsible for this kind of thing. At least I, for one, decline to believe that the first thing he does on arriving at his hotel or villa is to ring up the local Press and say: "Bernard Shaw speaking. I am swimming to-morrow; kindly send photographer." The pictures appear simply because the ubiquitous press photographer makes it his infernal business to be there and take them, because he and his Editor know that we, you and I, want them and like them and expect them, and Shaw, always ready to oblige, smilingly submits. This surely must be the explanation of Monday's picture—Bernard Shaw Swimming Breast

Stroke; or Tuesday's—Bernard Shaw Floating. By Wednesday he has turned on his side—Bernard Shaw Swimming Side Stroke; and by Thursday he has sub-merged—Bernard Shaw Swimming Under Water. Friday finds him standing on a raft in a pair of bathing drawers. Saturday—Bernard Shaw Drying Himself, and Sunday, completing, for the moment, this strange eventful history, a photograph of Bernard Shaw—Dry.

Until we let him alone we have only ourselves to blame. When at Adelphi Terrace an enterprising burglar induced Mrs. Shaw to put up at a bend in the beautiful Adams' staircase a grill made of iron spikes, Shaw's comment was that though any burglar could get over it it would come in handy to keep reporters out. A conceited man would keep open house for the Press.

This is all very well, you say, but there is no escap-ing the fact that many of Shaw's remarks as they appear in his Prefaces, interviews and articles *are* con-ceited. I think we can escape it easily, or rather there is no need to escape it, because the words in the last sentence, "as they appear," of themselves clear Shaw of conceit. The remarks as they appear in print are not as he made them; they lack immensely two things, the manner and tone of their delivery. For the true flavor of his remarks what he says is not more important than how he says it, and when they are tossed off lightly and rapidly in a soft Irish accent

with a whimsical twinkle of the eye, they appear not
as they do in cold print, the intolerable assertions of
an egomaniac, but as they really are, the sincere un-
affected words of a quick mind, a brilliantly humorous
talker, and a very charming and courteous man
whom, you suspect, nothing but humbug can anger.
For, in spite of all the brogue and twinkle, Shaw is
fundamentally sincere and means every word he says.
And for this very reason—recognizing something of
his own powers, he holds a very good opinion of
himself; not to do so would make him guilty of that
very humbug he has made it his special pleasure to
scourge. So that when Shaw ends an argument in
which the widening breach makes further fighting
impossible with the words "I assert my intellectual
superiority, that is all," while some people may raise
the old cry of Conceit! I, personally, perceive in these
words only the candid opinion of a man who is honest
enough to think that he's right and t'other man
wrong, and to say so, and I fancy most of us must
prefer this kind of fighting manliness, rare as it is,
to the usual insincere modesty that crawls around on
its belly toadying for equally insincere compliments.

HAS BERNARD SHAW CHANGED?

Having dealt with the first of our three questions, we now come to the second. It is the idlest question of the three, but had better be answered if for no other reason than that people never weary of asking it. They assume he *has* changed. He hasn't! His views are no more and no less respectable now than they ever were. In the first place why, pray, should he change them? He has always been perfectly happy with the ones he has got. Nothing has happened in the world to make him change them; on the contrary, everything has served to confirm them. His opinions have been vindicated and his prophecies fulfilled. In the second place, how, how could he possibly change, being what he is—a mystic? One of the penalties (or joys, according to the way of thinking) of being a mystic is that you don't and can't change your views. If you did you would no longer be a mystic. You can change the way you express your views, of course, and your expression of them may grow and flower into all manner of beauty and abundance, but that is not quite the same thing. The mystic arrives at his philosophy of life not by laborious calculations and reasoning, step by step, but by divination. Now divination is an immediate, instinctive, feminine process, arrived at without effort and almost unconsciously—a vision that breaks on one and comes one knows not where from or why. The man of reason, on the other hand, like H. G. Wells, who wants to be a philosopher and critic of life, must tabulate the facts of his experience and learning and add the long column of them up, figure to figure and fact to fact, until he gets the answer; whereas to the mystic the answer is known at the outset, and what he has to do is not an addition sum but a jig-saw puzzle, fitting the facts of his experience and learning into the vision revealed to him aforetime. The mystic's picture may be no nearer the absolute truth than the man of reason's sum; but it stands as good a chance of being, for at least it cannot go wrong through faulty addition. It is, therefore, the man of reason who is always growing and modifying his outlook and altering the total of his sum. But the mystic, because it is not his to alter, is perforce content with his original vision, and spends his days examining it from one angle after another. In short, the man of reason grows by discovering new things, while the mystic, denied growth, can but interpret or express things both old and new that he has known forever. G. K. Chesterton once said that he could lie awake at night and hear H. G. Wells growing. No one could ever say this of Shaw, who stands serene and pat on his first threshold. The knowledge that his vision is not of his own making saves him a certain amount of trouble, for he need not bother to explain it, even to himself. After the first night of *Heartbreak House,* on being asked what a certain passage meant, Shaw replied: "How should I know? I'm only the author." A kernel of deep truth in a shell of airy wit, as usual.

If the foregoing be true, we should find this change-lessness of Shaw reflected in his works. And that is what we do. Exactly the same anti-romanticism which he preached last century and embodied in his Swiss chocolate soldier of *Arms and the Man* appears forty years later in *Saint Joan,* which ends not in a melodramatic glow of flames from the stake, but with an anti-romantic top hat from Rome. Exactly the same philosophy which he gave us in *Man and Super-man* appears twenty years later in *Back to Methuselah.* The difference is one not of substance but degree, the furrows of conviction having but deepened the philos-ophy into a religion; Lilith succeeds Don Juan, but they both say the same thing—the Man more prac-tically, the Woman more mystically. It is the same with every trait, habit and conviction of the man. His anti-militarism started I don't know how many years ago when he first refused to eat animals or pluck flowers, and we have still to find him wearing a carnation in his buttonhole and eating beefsteaks. When he was obscure and struggling and red-bearded and had nothing to lose, he helped to found the Socialist Fabian Society; now, when he is famous, rich and white-bearded, he toils writing his *Intelligent Woman's Guide to Socialism and Capitalism* in order to endorse and impress upon us those same Fabian doctrines. It is, of course, politically that people like to think Bernard Shaw has changed, and become respectable and conservative, but do what he will Shaw finds it almost impossible to convince them that he is as he was, a revolutionary. Only a short time ago he was speaking from some platform when a man in the audience, red with anger, shook his finger at Shaw, and asked: "Are you, or are you not, a Bolshevist?" Shaw, instead of retorting indignantly with the evasion or negative which his heckler undoubtedly expected, folded his arms, smiled benignly and said, "I am a Bolshevist." At the appearance of *The Intelligent Woman's Guide* the majority of people reacted in three main ways. Some behaved as though someone had hiccoughed in polite society for a joke; that is, they disregarded it and went on conversing about the weather. Others, who read the book and took the author's sincerity for granted, felt that an elderly gentleman's solecism committed in his senility ought, after all, to be forgiven; while the rest, just because the author had been considerate enough to make his exceedingly long book readable by sprinkling a heavy theme with wit and leavening a ton of text with an ounce of humor, got out of their embarrassment by seeing nothing in the book but a leg-pull, and by answering our third question, therefore, *Is Bernard Shaw Serious?*, with a more emphatic negative than ever.

The fact that Shaw has had the good fortune to make some money, and has the good sense to use and enjoy whatever facilities of the modern world he fancies, seems to blind people to the fact that he can at the same time and with a quiet conscience hold perfectly sincere political opinions which, had he power to put them into effect, would change the order of society. Shaw cannot perform miracles and he very wisely doesn't try to. Having given it as his opinion that it would be about as easy to get scrambled eggs from a sewing-machine as Socialism from the present Labor Party, he is content to live as happily as he can in a society whose structure he disagrees with, and to make the best of a bad job. Some Bolshevists made the same mistake about Anatole France. They journeyed all the way to Paris to enlist his help, confident of the sympathy of one who had lashed Church and Finance and all the other pillars of society with such Olympian calm and gusto. But while they were waiting for the Frenchman to appear they were so overcome by the evidence of wealth and culture which they saw all around them as they stood in the anteroom that they bolted precipitately back to Russia without having seen him.

Shaw himself is as anxious as anyone to dispel the illusion that he has become respectable, because he says such a myth is bad for the sale of his works. "Nobody reads me," he laments; "they all regard me as a classic and treat me like an archbishop." And maybe it is true that Shaw is losing some of his power of irritating the public until it takes notice of him; if so it is a serious matter, for it is no paradox to say that Bernard Shaw, by one of those swings of the pendulum that whole generations are heir to, owes his present popularity to his past unpopularity. In any case I do not imagine that Shaw craves for popularity or thrives on it, and just as he realized that Saint Joan's power was at its height when the churchmen called her a heretic and the soldiers burnt her, so I imagine he wrote feelingly when he made the Maid say: "Woe unto me when all men praise me!"

Bernard Shaw has not changed. All his ideas are facets of his one first vision; all his plays form a cycle of mystical faith in which he proclaims, as we shall see in a moment, that each one of us is a Man of Destiny, a servant of the Life Force, and a temple of the Holy Ghost. If ever he were in need of help to keep his flag flying, perhaps the best help would be to insist, in the words of Mr. Collis, that whereas Shaw's beard was formerly red-hot with anger now it is white-hot with rage.

IS BERNARD SHAW SERIOUS?

THIS is probably the most burning question of the three, setting father against son and mother against daughter. From what has been said already we should not be surprised to find that everyone answers this question with a "No." On the other hand, you will be right if you think I am going to suggest that it should be answered with an unqualified "Yes." Bernard Shaw could hardly be clearer or more unequivocal on the subject. Take the following quotations, for example: "I care only for my mission as I call it, and my work." "No doubt I must recognize, as even the Ancient Mariner did, that I must tell my story entertainingly if I am to hold the wedding guest spellbound in spite of the siren sounds of the loud bassoon. But 'for art's sake' alone I would not face the toil of writing a single sentence." "Art for Art's sake is not enough." "No doubt that literary knack of mine which happens to amuse the British public distracts attention from my character; but the character is there none the less, solid as bricks." "My conscience is the genuine pulpit article; it annoys me to see people comfortable when they ought to be uncomfortable; and I insist on making them think in order to bring them to conviction of sin."

These remarks of Shaw's are typical of his efforts to make people take him seriously and understand him. What more can he do or say? Whether we believe him is, of course, a matter for us to decide, but if we choose not to, we must face the fact that we are deliberately disbelieving a man who has made it his special province to tell the truth about the world and the people in it, as he sees it, unvarnished, and to tell it more unaffectedly, more unreservedly, more unceasingly than probably any other person alive to-day.

What is the trouble, then? Why is not Bernard Shaw taken as seriously as, say, the Florentines took Savonarola? The reason is obvious, I think. For while Shaw is always serious, he is never solemn, and for some obscure reason we are loath to believe that anyone can mean what he says unless he pulls a long face while saying it. Wit! That, in one word, is Shaw's trouble, just as it has been his salvation. Savonarola, not being a witty man, was burnt alive by those whom his unbuttoned rapier hurt. Shaw, on the other hand, confesses that his mother wit has many a time saved him from the stake's modern equivalent. But this escape has had to be paid for, and in Shaw's case the price was high, for he has had to suffer the preacher's anguish of preaching not to an empty church but to a packed congregation of deaf persons.

The essential purpose of Shaw is to administer mental and spiritual purgatives, and what do the ungrateful patients do but suck the sugar off and then spit out the pill? Here, again, Shaw is to blame, for the sugar of his wit is so lavish that it forms a meal by itself, so that audiences who attend his plays find primarily entertainments where they are offered primarily sermons. And such entertainments! Ask one of these audiences and to a man and woman they will swear they have got more laughter and fun out of a Shaw play than if they had gone to see the latest musical comedy or farce. But not more than one per cent of them, if they are honest, will confess to appreciating and digesting more than the sugar; that alone was worth the price of admission. True, they paid for the pill, the author's heart's blood, but let it go! What matter so long as they have had their money's worth! Poor Shaw! The scene that goes best in *Candida* is the episode of Prossy tipsy; *Caesar and Cleopatra* is remembered chiefly for Sir Johnston Forbes Robertson; *Pygmalion* for its "Bloody"; *Mrs. Warren's Profession* for being banned so long; *Fanny's First Play* for the trimmings of its critics; while to many *Arms and the Man* is only the unmusical version of *The Chocolate Soldier*.

When Shaw protested against the artificial romantic play by supplanting its stained-glass heroes and virtuous heroines and wholetime villains with a touch of nature, and concocted plays out of the natural ingredients of the human drama, where weakness and strength, viciousness and good feelings struggle together in the same breast, he dumfounded his audiences. Theatergoers had accepted stagey characters for so long that when human beings were offered them on the stage they refused to take them seriously. Surely the author was joking? Well, if we want to put it that way, we can, for, says Bernard Shaw in the words of Peter Keegan, "My way of joking is to tell the truth: it's the funniest joke in the world." Similarly we can answer those who accuse him of always pulling people's legs: "True, he does; but only because he thinks they're crooked."

There is a further point in this matter of Shaw himself being to blame. Quite recently he has confessed his inability to sustain his periods of tragic writing beyond a certain point. At that point a seemingly irresistible impulse seizes him at the height of his power and persuades him to end the period of deep feeling with a joke. We remember how Sir James Barrie describes the way his plays come to be written; how the work-a-day Barrie sits, pen in hand, and after a while there comes another being, distinct yet within himself, who takes charge of the situation and with Barrie's pen traces his most delicate whimsicalities. Sir James feels indebted enough to his elf to give it a name, calling it McConnachie. Shaw's imp, on the other hand, has not been christened, not publicly at any rate, and I doubt whether its begetter feels indebted to it at all. No sooner has the Tragic Muse called at Mr. Shaw's than his imp insists on her being shown the door, with the result that even his unpleasant plays are such good fun that he has specially to label them Unpleasant. An example of this imp's activities which of course sport through all the plays in a ravage of leavening and lightening is seen clearly in Caesar's address to the Sphinx in *Caesar and Cleopatra*. It is the first meeting between Cleopatra and Caesar. The moonlit stillness of the desert, the two human beings alone and far from their followers, these things are a setting of grave beauty, and, fitly enough, Caesar's words keep to the high level of the setting. But the moment a chance comes, Shaw and Cleopatra seize it with both hands and with a joke topple over both speech and setting as though what had been built up sublimely was nothing more than a house of cards. It may be worth while to quote the whole passage, seeing that it will do a double duty, not only illustrating the point under discussion but also revealing, as I see it, something almost autobiographical of Shaw, a man serious, mystical, essentially alone.

Caesar: Hail Sphinx: salutation from Julius Caesar! I have wandered in many lands, seeking the lost regions from which my birth into this world exiled me, and the company of such creatures as I myself. I have found flocks and pastures, men and cities, but no other Caesar, no air native to me, no man kindred to me, none who can do my day's deed, and think my night's thought. In the little world yonder, Sphinx, my place is as high as yours in this great desert; only I wander and you sit still; I conquer, and you endure; I work and wonder, you watch and wait; I look up and am dazzled, look down and am darkened, look round and am puzzled, whilst your eyes never turn from looking out—out of the world—to the lost region—the home from which we have strayed. Sphinx, you and I, strangers to the race of men, are no strangers to one another: have I not been conscious of you and of this place since I was born? Rome is a madman's dream; this is my Reality. These starry lamps of yours I have seen from afar in Gaul, in Britain, in Spain, in Thessaly, signaling great secrets to some eternal sentinel below, whose post I never could find. And here at last is their sentinel: an image of the constant and immortal part of my life, silent, full of thoughts, alone in the silver desert. Sphinx, Sphinx: I have climbed mountains at night to hear in the distance the stealthy footfall of the winds that chase your sands in forbidden play: our invisible children, O Sphinx, laughing in whispers. My way hither was the way of destiny; for I am he of whose genius you are the symbol: part brute, part woman, part god: nothing of man in me at all. Have I read your riddle, Sphinx?

Cleopatra: (who, hidden in a paw of the Sphinx, has wakened and peeped cautiously from her nest to see who is speaking) Old gentleman.

THE SHAVIAN ESSENCE

HAVING tried to convince my readers that Bernard Shaw is not conceited but honest, that he is the same now as he has always been, and that he is serious and sincere, the next step follows naturally. What is it that this honest and serious and sincere man is so honest and serious and sincere about? What, briefly, is Bernard Shaw's message, what are his convictions and faith? Unluckily we can do no more than touch in passing this core and heart of our subject, but luckily Shaw is concise and explicit on the point. Before hearing him, however, let us be quite sure that we understand the meaning of the words "moral" and "morality" as he uses them. Shaw attaches to these words not their vulgar specialized meaning concerning the relations between the sexes in particular, but their full true meaning concerning human habits, customs, conventions and institutions in general. Thus a moral man is not simply one who forbears to run off with somebody else's wife; he is one who abides by the general rules and follows the general customs which the laws and institutions of his time and country seek to impose on him. When Shaw therefore declares himself a "moral revolutionary" he is not hoisting the libertine's flag; he is simply declaring war on all custom which has not the sanction of conscience; on all habit which is the fruit of either a false perception of life or a refusal to face it; on all laws which, however just and beneficial formerly, have outgrown the conditions for which they were framed; on all institutions which shut their eyes to, or support and enforce the state of affairs resulting from such customs, habits and laws. The reader will say that if such be the case, a moral revolutionary has his work cut out. Yet, there is hardly a relationship or activity of civilization —I cannot think of one—which Shaw has not at one time or another attacked: medical, marital, religious, sexual, militaristic, dynastic, artistic, national, international, social, educational, historical, municipal and diplomatic, and he has not retired yet.

Shaw's foes are the people who do a thing because "it's done" or "it's the thing to do," without thought, and them he belabors mercilessly, because, as he very properly points out, by acting with fashion or custom instead of with conscience for guide, they have no means of knowing how disastrous the consequences of their unconsidered actions may be to their fellows and posterity, let alone themselves. Thus this following for fashion's sake alone makes humbugs of us all, and it is from this tyranny and spiritual sapping that Shaw would deliver us, even as a good forester would strip a tree of the ivy strangling it. When Shaw contemplates us in this way we are to him not twentieth century creatures as distinct from nineteenth century, nor Anglo-Saxons as distinct from Slavs or Latins (his first acclamation was in Germany and the first world production of *The Apple Cart* took place in Poland), nor as rich men with university education as distinct from poor men with state elementary education,—he regards us as none of these—but simply as specimens of the *genus homo,* naked, unashamed, natural, unhumbugged, each one of us given a chance by God.

This will perhaps help us to grasp better Shaw's own unequivocal declaration. In a letter to the late H. M. Hyndman, Bernard Shaw wrote: "I am a moral revolutionary, interested, not in class war, but in the struggle between human vitality and the artificial system of morality, and distinguishing not between capitalist and proletarian, but between moralist and natural historian." That is all. The fight, in short, is Conscience *versus* Custom, with Shaw fighting for the former. Referring to what one might call Shaw's continuous guerilla actions, William James said: "To me, Shaw's great service is the way he brings home to the *eyes,* as it were, the difference between convention and conscience, and the way he shows that you can tell the truth successfully if you will only keep benignant enough while doing it."

It will readily be gathered that to be a moral revolutionary requires an able mind in order to analyze the conventions of civilization and frame therefrom one's revolutionary tenets, and a strong character in order to be able to maintain the latter cheerfully and fearlessly in the teeth of personal unpopularity and the deadweight of custom. It is not a rôle for the weak or selfish. Even happiness goes by the board as no longer worthy of pursuit. In *Candida* Marchbanks, suddenly grown up, declares: "I no longer desire happiness: life is nobler than that." Similarly Napoleon in *The Man of Destiny* says: "Happiness is the most tedious thing in the world to me. Should I be what I am if I cared about happiness?" Remember, too, in *Man and Superman* that it is the Devil who, a leader of the best society and a perfect gentleman, does nothing but try to keep his subjects contented with happiness in Hell, where there is nothing to do except enjoy oneself.

Behind every fight is a faith, and the greater a man's faith the better he will fight. The faith which sustains Bernard Shaw is a belief in Creative Evolution or, as he alternatively calls it, the Life Force. The summary of this faith or religion is as follows: "There is a spiritual power in the Universe; call it the Life Force. About its origin we know nothing. It is neither all-powerful nor all-knowing, but strives to become both through its own expressions and creations. It goes slowly forward by trial and error. Man is the latest trial. He may be an error. But he is not a base accident of nature." If an error, man as we know him will be scrapped, and something else tried; but it may be within man's power so to subserve the Life Force that he shall survive and be used for further divine experiments and gropings. If we turn to the end of *Back to Methuselah* we shall find an exquisite poem, though not in meter, with which Shaw ends his five-play-Pentateuch of faith. When the curtain falls one expects to hear the roll of cosmic drums. The ghosts of Adam and Eve have appeared and spoken and faded away, and Lilith, who was before Adam and Eve, speaks.

"They have accepted the burden of Eternal Life. . . . Best of all, they are still not satisfied: the impulse I gave them in that day when I sundered myself in twain and launched Man and Woman on the earth still urges them: after passing a million goals they press on to the goal of redemption from the flesh, to the vortex freed from matter, to the whirlpool in pure intelligence that, when the world began, was a whirlpool in pure force. And though all that they have done seems but the first hour of the infinite work of creation, yet I will not supersede them until they have forded this last stream that lies between flesh and spirit, and disentangled their life from the matter that has always mocked it. I can wait: waiting and patience mean nothing to the eternal. I gave the woman the greatest of gifts: curiosity. By that her seed has been saved from my wrath; for I also am curious; and I have waited always to see what they will do to-morrow. Let them feed that appetite well for me. I say, let them dread, of all things, stagnation; for from the moment I, Lilith, lose hope and faith in them, they are doomed. In that hope and faith I have let them live for a moment; and in that moment I have spared them many times. But mightier creatures than they have killed hope and faith, and perished from the earth; and I may not spare them forever. I am Lilith: I brought life into the whirlpool of force, and compelled my enemy, Matter, to obey a living soul. But in enslaving Life's enemy I made him Life's master; for that is the end of all slavery; and now I shall see the slave set free and the enemy reconciled, the whirlpool become all life and no matter. . . .

"Of Life only is there no end; and though of its million starry mansions many are empty and many still unbuilt, and though its vast domain is as yet unbearably desert, my seed shall one day fill it and master its matter to the uttermost confines. And for what is beyond, the eyesight of Lilith is too short. It is enough that there *is* a beyond."

The Life Force is too impersonal and nebulous a conception for many of us to make a religion of it. But can we reject Shaw's definition of the religious as those who feel that they are the instruments of a

Power and Purpose which far transcends their mere personal selves and embraces the universe? Is he not appealing to our religious emotion when he invites us to offer ourselves joyously to the Life Force, for it to experiment with? To pull and push and strive forward, gropingly, but as best we may, away from matter and towards spirit, our conscience our only guide: this is the ecstasy of Creative Evolution. "This," cries Bernard Shaw through his Don Juan, "This is the true joy of life: the being used for a purpose recognized by yourself as a mighty one; the being thoroughly worn out before you are thrown on the scrapheap; the being a force of nature, instead of a feverish selfish little clod of ailments and grievances, complaining that the world will not devote itself to making you happy." And again: "I tell you that as long as I can conceive something better than myself I cannot be easy unless I am striving to bring it into existence or clearing the way for it. That is the law of my life."

Work! Nothing else matters. Work! All the other things will be added unto you. "I must take myself as I am and get what work I can out of myself." And let your work be dictated by your conscience and not embarked on with an eye to fame, so that it be acceptable to the Life Force. Referring to *Widowers' Houses* Bernard Shaw remarks: "I heartily hope that the time will come when this play will be both utterly impossible and utterly unintelligible." The evils of landlordism existed: that was enough for Shaw to try to expose them; but that his exposure should beget him literary fame, now or after, was a matter that never crossed his busy mind. As with literary immortality, so with personal immortality. It does not interest him any more than death frightens him. "I am looking," he says, "for a race of men who are not afraid of death," himself believing that the spark within him at death returns to the main stream of Life to "renew the battalions of the future."

THE THING ABOUT BERNARD SHAW

The thing that strikes one about Bernard Shaw is his good temper. Probably no one has fought more fights in his time; yet I do not remember a single occasion on which he has lost his temper in one of them. Always he gives the impression of being furious with the sin and on the most friendly terms with the sinner. One feels that the real Shaw is speaking through Julius Caesar when he makes him cry: "Resent! Oh thou foolish Egyptian, what have I to do with resentment?"

If I were forced to describe Bernard Shaw in one word I should choose the word "serene." To me he is the serenest young old man alive, and this quality seems to radiate from him as a kind of mental glow which permeates all his activities. Because of it he himself acts on those he meets like the sunshine he advocates, and even meeting him in the talkies is a tonic. In advertisements you will see pictures of people who are paid to say that they have become serene through eating a certain food or drinking a certain drink; this kind of serenity, induced from without by calories or vitamins, is not Shaw's kind. His is the marrow of his being, and is the cause rather than the result of his surprising health. We can be quite sure that vegetarian diet never produced the serenity, but it is more than likely that the serenity persuaded Shaw to a vegetarian diet. Derived thus from spiritual health and mental outlook this thread of serenity never wears out and serves its owner in all manner of ways. It enables Shaw to deal calmly and dispassionately with situations of which he remains imperturbable master where others would feel embarrassed, if not in actual danger. For example, as Shaw stood on the stage before an enthusiastically applauding house to make his speech at the first night of *Arms and the Man,* a heroic youth in the gallery waited for the silence and then broke it with a piercing hiss. Like a flash and not discomfited at all, Bernard Shaw was able to fix the man with a broad smile and shout back: "Sir, I quite agree with you; but what can we two do against a whole houseful of the opposite opinion?"

Similarly Shaw can criticize in a way that gives no offense and yet leaves nothing more to be said. Thus while attending a fashionable musicale in his professional capacity he was asked by a too gushing hostess what he thought of the new violinist she had unearthed. Beaming, Shaw said he reminded him of Paderewski. After a moment's very natural hesitation the nonplussed hostess ventured to suggest to the great critic that Paderewski was not a violinist, and Shaw acquiesced with a "Just so! Just so!"

As with criticism, so with compliments. Call it blarney, wit, genius, cheek, serenity or what you will, their subtle bouquet holds. Some time ago Shaw asked a certain actress to play again the part of Candida which she had played so beautifully before. The lady wrote saying she was sorry, but that since the last production of the play she had married and couldn't leave her small boy; whereupon Shaw, unlike so many managers who would have implied that there were just as good fish in the sea, wrote back on a postcard (he is always writing postcards): "Damn you, madam, you have ruined my play: I hope your boy grows up to be an actor."

Conversely Bernard Shaw is an adept at rapping people over the knuckles if he thinks they deserve it. There is the story of Shaw and a beautiful lady (often erroneously identified with the late Isadora Duncan). She had written to the famous writer pointing out that he had the finest brain and she the finest body in the world and proposing, for the sake of posterity, that they should unite to produce a wonderchild inheriting her beauty and his brains. This was too much for the author of *Man and Superman* and creator of Ann Whitefield, and Shaw replied, on a postcard as usual, "Ah; but suppose it were to inherit my beauty and your brains!"

I have no means of verifying these stories either in their main or in their details. When *Arms and the*

Man had its first night I wasn't born; I wasn't at the musicale and its hostess is probably now no more; and I don't read postcards and letters unless addressed to myself. Perhaps Mr. Shaw will put us right on the stories if I have given them to you wrongly, for he is a stickler for accuracy. I only know that they are current. Even if they never happened at all they ought to, and in any case Shaw must learn to suffer legends to grow around him, as he suffers so many things, serenely. He cannot have it *all* his own way.

BERNARD SHAW AND AMERICA

No account, however brief, of a man so much concerned with the future of man and so intent upon projecting himself mentally into that future would be just and complete without an effort to appraise Bernard Shaw's relations with the continent of North America, that land upon whose success or failure, rise or fall, the future of western civilization probably depends.

Bernard Shaw has never been to America: but that does not mean he never will. It would be just like him to surprise two hemispheres by crossing the Atlantic just when the world's wager was a thousand chances to one against his doing so. The position, largely analogous to his refusal for so long to broadcast to America, is as follows. He declined a succession of invitations to broadcast because he said he could think of nothing that would be of mutual interest to himself and his American listeners-in. If therefore he contracted to broadcast a speech upon a subject interesting to Americans but not to himself his fee would be a million dollars for five minutes. The exact figures of the fee and the time do not matter; Shaw's only object was to make further negotiations impossible by making his terms gloriously and exorbitantly prohibitive. Perhaps it is needless to add that he achieved his object, and that all negotiations on this basis were dropped like so many hot bricks; just as Shaw intended. But, he was always careful to say, with his twinkle well in evidence, that if ever he came across a subject which interested him and which he judged would also interest Americans, he would be delighted to broadcast a speech on that subject to America for nothing. In good time the subject appeared. It was Einstein. Accordingly Bernard Shaw spoke on the air for the first time to North America. It behoves us therefore if we are wise to be wary of wagering that he will or will not come to America. If he finds anything of sufficient interest to him in America to do or see or hear he will come; and do it or see it or hear it and go home again, like the practical, busy, sensible person he is. In other words, he will come to America if he wants to. But he will not be bribed.

Shaw himself has given n reasons why he does not come to America, and the reasons given by others, some of them authorized and some of them unauthorized, are m. Authorized and unauthorized, they vary between a fear of seasickness and the subtle showmanship of a Bolingbroke by which the showman in Shaw realizes that Richard II played his cards badly, and that the greater the distance kept between the public and its idol the deeper will be that public's genuflexions. Indeed when the distance is virtually infinite and comprises a frontier of water 3,000 miles wide dividing not only two continents but two worlds, the Old and the New, then genuflexion is a lame word indeed to describe the public's delighted grovelling. Not only is its knee bent, but its nose is rubbing the dust, its whole body imitating the posture of a Moslem at sunset. It is also the posture most boys assume under compulsion in the headmaster's study during their school days. Shaw definitely likes people in this posture, for out he whips his bastinado and gives his worshipper a resounding smack on the (in this position) uppermost part of the latter's anatomy. Unlike the case of the delinquent schoolboy, however, Shaw's bastinado produces not tears but only gurgles and giggles of delight in its prostrate victim, and the more he rubs the American public's nose in the dust the broader becomes the grin on its gladly suffering face. For example, *The Apple Cart's* American audiences laughed more loudly than perhaps at any other moment in the play when Lysistrata (Ly Sistrata, as Shaw points out, and not Lysis Trata) says, "What we call an American is only a Wop pretending to be a Pilgrim Father." Yet this is really less disparaging than his much earlier description of the United States as a Nation of Villagers, capable of producing heroic sub-postmistresses and blacksmiths, but unconscious of anything ten miles away, or than his later definition of the hundred per cent American as ninety-nine per cent idiot. Worst of all, perhaps, is his explanation that such descriptions apply to every nation on earth, but that the American is conceited enough to think that he is the only fool in the world, and takes them as personal insults accordingly, though Mr. Sinclair Lewis, with his Babbits and Gantries, has won the Nobel prize by being harder on his countrymen than fifty Shaws.

The modern analysts why pry into our souls and find only neuroses there might say that an American who laughs when he hears or reads these pen-portraits of himself is indulging in mental self-flagellation; I prefer to be more old-fashioned and say that he has a sense of humor; which can perhaps be defined worse than as "the ability to laugh at oneself." Nevertheless the possession or otherwise of a sense of humor by the victim does not alter the conduct of the tormentor. How shall we defend the writing of such a line by Shaw who when he wrote it had not so much as set foot in the country whose inhabitants he was criticizing with such sting? Even Caesar had the grace to come and see before he conquered. Shaw presumes to criticize without even coming and seeing. Well, in the first place, the line does succeed in making everyone, Americans included, laugh; and Shaw knew it would. Secondly, the line is not without a kernel of truth: if this be disputed, let someone else try to define an American better in twelve words, the definition to be a critical and not a dictionary or milk and water one. Thirdly, as always the context must be considered: and we find there that the line is spoken by a Powermistress General who has a way of saying just exactly what she thinks, and bluntly, and who proudly says, "I am English: every bone in my body." Shaw as dramatist can shift the burden of the line on to the broad shoulders of Lysistrata and disclaim all responsibility. In any case, there it is! Americans will console themselves in the contemplation of England which has suffered and thriven upon half a century of Shavian torment, and still survives. After all, to be selected for the application of the Shavian bastinado (not his whip, though, which makes no one laugh) is in itself no mean compliment. Like England, America finds that the only thing to do is to grin and bear it.

One of the most interesting reasons why Bernard Shaw will not come to America as so many other men of letters come, on a sponsored and paid lecture tour, is because he would break a lifelong rule if he did so. Never has Shaw accepted a penny for his public speaking, which fact alone should quash and kill forever the idea in the heads of many people that in money matters Shaw is grasping in the proverbial Scotch or Jewish sense. Bernard Shaw is not grasping: he is businesslike. He declines to be imposed upon, and he will not allow others to make money out of him without demanding, and seeing to it that he receives, a fair quid pro quo. Shaw is both human and humane when deciding upon that quid pro quo's justness and fairness. The manner in which this particular rule of Shaw's became established derives from the early days of Shaw the freethinker, when the handsome red-bearded young man began to be noticed, and invitations to speak and debate on this vexed question and that began to find their way to his desk. They all said the same thing: fee ten guineas, politics and religion barred. Shaw always answered that he never spoke in public on anything except politics and religion, but that if the club or society would waive this condition, he, on his part, would willingly waive his fee and be content financially with an imbursement of a third class return railway fare if the length of the journey were out of the ordinary.

Yet, in spite of Bernard Shaw's persistence in declining to parade in person in the United States of America and Canada, is there anyone who, over a period of years, is better known in these two countries? Presidents come and Presidents go, but Shaw goes on forever. Similarly in Canada, Governor-Generals and Prime Ministers fill the public eye, but only for their tenure of office. They are men of the moment, but how quickly the moment is over! The stock of Shaw's publicity, on the other hand, mounts

steadily: it pays compound interest. The factory of
his publicity is constantly adding new wings and
installing new equipment, and with the aid of these
Bernard Shaw the myth is shipped across the Atlantic,
massed and syndicated, while Bernard Shaw the man
sits snug at home. For many years the stock in trade
of Shaw's publicity was restricted to his plays, which
captured theatergoers, his pamphlets which captured
freethinkers and advanced thinkers, and his interviews which captured newspaper readers. Whether
the capture of these large sections of the public re-
sulted in firing fury and irritation in their breasts as
well as adoration does not matter: the point is that
all of them were captured. More recently, taking ad-
vantage of scientific inventions, Shaw has been able
to enlarge the equipment of his publicity plant. He
has used the movie, the talkie and the radio as medi-
ums for revealing his own personality; he has super-
vised the turning of some of his plays into talkies;
while alongside the inauguration of these mechani-
calities there has gone on a steady increment in the
vogue and understanding of his plays, until to-day
there are in England, Canada and the United States
accredited theatrical companies which play his works
either continuously or regularly year after year. The
company in England has earned the nickname of The
Pit Ponies, its seasons are so long and so seldom does
it "come up to the surface."

The first two talkies which Bernard Shaw made
of himself and which have been round the world are
intimate and self-revelatory to a degree that only Shaw
could carry off with honors. Successfully and per-
ilously he performs the extraordinarily difficult feat
of making a fool of himself without once making
himself either cheap or ridiculous. Brimming over
with playful boast yet entirely devoid of conceit he
serenely commands his audience of millions to note
the Shakespearean cast of his brow and begs them, as
he turns slowly on his own axis to behold his north-
ern, southern, eastern and western aspects. It is all
great fun and part of his serenity: he draws us all
with him into the upper air of that serenity where
it is difficult to be cheap and impossible to be dull.

A very different note pervaded Shaw's first broadcast to America, but it too was a self-revelatory one.
In it he claimed kinship with Einstein whom he was
having the honor to introduce at a banquet in London. On what grounds did Shaw claim kinship to
the maker of our latest universe? Shaw is not a
scientist. Was it on the common ground of genius,
or of intellect, or iconoclasm, or freethought? On
none of these. Shaw claimed kinship with Einstein
because he said both of them experienced, each in his
sphere, a great solitude, each had achieved a peak of
loneliness. And the man in whom the world at large
sees nothing but a cynic, scoffer, wit and buffoon went

on to speak of "the secret places of the heart." It is in those place that the real Bernard Shaw lives: they are not open to the public. If they were, the public, like sheep, like mountain sheep, would scramble up the peak of his loneliness and cluster gaping and hustling, leaving their litter of paper and orange peel around, depriving the man of the precious calm of a solitude that is neither tragic nor comic, but only real.

When one thinks thus of Bernard Shaw there intrudes gently and without bathos the picture of another man who has made the whole world of our generation laugh: Charlie Chaplin, a man of genius too. For Chaplin, like Shaw, is a perfectly serious person. The difference between them in this respect is that while the secret places of Shaw's heart are locked to the public Chaplin's are open, admission free. We have to call him Charles now and drop the Charlie; he means us to be impressed by the kind of music with which he solaces himself and the kind of literature that appeals to him; he lets it be known that one of his greatest ambitions is to play Hamlet, and would doubtless jump at the chance of playing Christ in a Passion Play. Shaw, on the other hand, in the public's eye and in his own alike, will be quite content to continue to play himself.

THE APPLE CART

Much, and perhaps enough, has been written about *The Apple Cart,* and this volume, which, if it has merits, must count its slender dimensions as one of them, is no place to succumb to the temptation of discussing any one play of Bernard Shaw's at any length. Rather, keeping in mind "The Real Bernard Shaw," let us see whether it is possible to trace a confirmation in this, Shaw's fortieth play, of our contentions that the author is a serious man, an unchanged man, a just man and a serene one. There is space for but a single item of evidence for each contention.

A serious man. It will be difficult, if indeed possible, to find anyone who can read or hear the impassioned speech of the Powermistress, in which she describes the methods of "Breakages, Limited," and who can deny the completely serious import of it and the equally serious intention and desire of the author to be taken seriously.

An unchanged man. The preface to the play speaks for itself and for Shaw. We can take it or leave it, believe him or disbelieve him, agree or disagree; but whichever we do we shall not have upset his stand.

For fifty years the winds from the four corners of the earth have blown upon the rock, bringing with them minute spores which have gradually clothed the rock with soft and delicate lichens, making it less stark, forbidding and jagged in appearance than when the sea first threw up the rock seventy years ago. But lichens, come their spores from Buckingham Palace or Moscow and be their efflorescence never so bearded and patriarchal, do not lessen the strength of the rock they flower on or change its position.

A just man. Queen Jemima thinks it a good thing for King Magnus to become Emperor of America because then, she says, the English can "civilize these Americans." If in the audience there is a narrow nationalist, a purveyor of what Shaw calls "patriotic songs, hatred of the foreigner, and guff and bugaboo," he or she will probably clap together his or her complacent mischief-making hands. It is just on such people that Shaw falls like a ton of bricks—only with more point and precision than bricks. With fair-mindedness and Olympian impartiality comes the answer of King Magnus Shaw: "How can we when we have not yet civilized ourselves?" The narrow nationalist who clapped but a moment before is silenced, and if wise and willing to learn can begin thenceforward to understand Bernard Shaw.

A serene man. It is perhaps enough to ask the question, "Could the creation of King Magnus pro-

ceed from a mind and being which was not quint-
essentially serene?"

Shaw has said categorically that it is no use people
taking his plays at their "suburban face value," and
that they will get out of them only what they bring
to them, adding in characteristic fashion, "which in
most cases is nothing." Shaw's plays are mines, and
we therefore have his authority for knowing, to our
satisfaction, that if we find nuggets the fact that they
are of gold is partly due to us. There are plenty for
each of us. Personally I am proud of finding two,
each of them a little nugget of autobiography, and
exemplifying one of the outstanding traits of Bernard
Shaw's character: his good manners. Here is one.

Magnus: If you may flourish your thunderbolts
why may I not shoulder my little popgun of a veto
and strut up and down with it for a moment?

Nicobar: This is not a subject for jesting—

Magnus (*interrupting him quickly*): I am not jesting, Mr. Nicobar. But I am certainly trying to discuss
our differences in a good humoured manner. Do you
wish me to lose my temper and make scenes?

And again, how comforting it would be, when pur-
sued against your will by a persistent wooer, both of
you moreover already married to other parties, to
know that you had the ability to reply and rebuke
in words as firm and clear and beautiful as those used

by Magnus to his favorite when he declines to accede to her request to drown or shoot or divorce his Queen.

Magnus: Do not let us fall into the common mistake of expecting to become one flesh and one spirit. Every star has its own orbit; and between it and its nearest neighbour there is not only a powerful attraction but an infinite distance. When the attraction becomes stronger than the distance the two do not embrace; they crash together in ruin. We two also have our orbits, and must keep an infinite distance between us to avoid a disastrous collision. Keeping our distance is the whole secret of good manners: and without good manners human society is intolerable and impossible.

Shaw's manners are more than "good"; they are instinctive and therefore beautiful: as beautiful as his hands.

WHEN THE TUMULT AND THE
SHOUTING DIES

IF a string of Shavian anecdotes or superficialities
would satisfy you, my task would be simple. I could
tell you, for instance, of Bernard Shaw's love of swimming; of his interest in boxing and his acquaintance
with Gene Tunney; of his leaning towards the mystical
philosophy of strength culture professed by the ex-
champion wrestler George Hackenschmidt; of how he
declined the money, a sum of £8,000 or nearly 40,000
dollars, when he was awarded the Nobel Prize (did
you know, by the way, that Nobel was the inventor of
dynamite?); of how it is reported that tradesmen make
more money by selling Shaw's weekly cheques for the
neat spidery signatures on them than by cashing them
in the ordinary way, and how Shaw could stop the
practice only by paying for his vegetables and groceries
in cash; of how the Royalist Society of the U.S.A.
(whatever that may be) voted Bernard Shaw King of
America and Will Rogers Vice-King; and so on. Let
us, however, plod on in our effort to probe to the heart
of our man.

This rich Bolshevik, this ascetic who insists that he is
a voluptuary and that all the conventional self-in-

dulgences are self-tortures, this relentless worker, this merry puritan, this Bernard Shaw who takes no drugs or drink or chewing gum or tobacco, confesses to one stimulant: he goes to church. Our eyebrows will lower themselves again when I add that Shaw's church is any church so long as it is empty. He has been heard to remark in the laughingly matter of fact tone he always instinctively adopts in order to hide his innermost feelings, that an empty cathedral is the one place he can go into and be at peace. There, one with God and with the beggar at the door alike, the man can dip into the well of his being and draw upon the still waters in its depths, depths where the bubbles of wit that break in laughter on the blown and shining surface have no place and where the actor can take off both the comic and the tragic mask and reach the other side of good and evil. Blake said, "Excess of sorrow laughs. Excess of joy weeps." In church Shaw does neither. It infuriates him to be sentimentalized as a tragic figure behind the scenes or when the audience isn't looking. We remember the story of Grimaldi, the great Italian clown. A certain man went to see a doctor because he was feeling depressed. The doctor examined him and finding him suffering from acute melancholia recommended him to go to the circus and see Grimaldi. *He* would cheer him up. The man smiled sadly and said, "But I am Grimaldi." Shaw at his sickest cures his doctors of melancholia.

Let us then leave Bernard Shaw, incongruous as it may seem, alone in his empty church with "broken bits of laughter stuck about his heart," as Godfrey Elton puts it. But see! the church is not empty after all. In the dim stained light is another figure; a man with the face of a young saint, yet with white hair; he stands in a trance gazing into the infinite. Why! it is Peter Keegan. Shaw will not mind his being there, a poor madman who harms nobody. Let us speak to him. We go over to him and like sightseers prod him with a question: what is he thinking of, we ask. He answers that he is dreaming of heaven. We press our vulgar curiosity and, with a picture in our minds of "a sort of pale blue satin place, with all the pious old ladies of the congregation sitting as if they were at a service, and some awful person in a study at the other end of the hall," we ask Mad Keegan what the heaven of *his* dreams is like. He replies: "In my dreams it is a country where the State is the Church and the Church the people: three in one and one in three. It is a commonwealth in which work is play and play is life: three in one and one in three. It is a temple in which the priest is the worshipper and the worshipper the worshipped: three in one and one in three. It is a godhead in which all life is human and all humanity divine: three in one and one in three. It is, in short, the dream of a madman."

If we wish to call Bernard Shaw mad, I do not think he will mind: he is in such good company.